FAMOUS ATHLETES

ELIZABETH RAUM

www.raintreepublishers.co.uk
Visit our website to find out more information about **Raintree** books.

To order:
☎ Phone 44 (0) 1865 888112
📄 Send a fax to 44 (0) 1865 314091
💻 Visit the Raintree bookshop at **www.raintreepublishers.co.uk** to browse our catalogue and order online.

First published in Great Britain by
Raintree, Halley Court, Jordan Hill,
Oxford OX2 8EJ, part of Harcourt
Education. Raintree is a registered
trademark of Harcourt Education Ltd.

Editorial: Melanie Waldron and Catherine Clarke
Design: Victoria Bevan and Bigtop
Picture Research: Hannah Taylor
Production: Julie Carter

Originated by Chroma Graphics Pte. Ltd
Printed and bound in China by Leo Paper Group

ISBN 978 1 4062 0683 8 (hardback)
12 11 10 09 08
10 9 8 7 6 5 4 3 2 1

ISBN 978 1 4062 0704 0 (paperback)
12 11 10 09 08
10 9 8 7 6 5 4 3 2 1

**British Library Cataloguing in
Publication Data**
Raum, Elizabeth
Famous athletes. – (Heroes or zeros?) (Atomic)
796
A full catalogue record for this book is available
from the British Library.

Acknowledgements
The publishers would like to thank the following for
permission to reproduce photographs: Corbis pp. **5**
(top) (Gideon Mendel), **6** (epa/John. G. Mabanglo), **17**
(Bettmann); Empics pp. **10** (bottom) (ABACA), **26** (top)
(AP), **26** (bottom) (AP); Getty Images pp. **5** (bottom)
(AFP/Adrian Dennis), **9** (Shaun Botterill), **10** (top) (AFP/
John Macdougall), **18** (AFP), **21** (top) (Simon Bruty),
21 (bottom) (Chris Cole), **22** (top), **22** (bottom) (Sean
Garnsworthy), **25** (Time Life Pictures/John Dominis), **29**
(Warren Little); NBAE (Getty Images) pp. **13** (bottom),
13 (top), **14**.

Cover photograph of Jennifer Capriati playing at the US
Open, 2004, reproduced with permission of Getty Images.

The publishers would like to thank Nancy Harris,
Diana Bentley, and Dee Reid for their assistance in the
preparation of this book.

Contents

Some words are printed in bold, **like this**. You can find out what they mean in the glossary. You can also look in the box at the bottom of the page where the word first appears.

FUN, FAME, AND FORTUNE

Many children participate in sport. Playing is fun – and so is winning! But some young athletes show particular skills or talents and may train harder and enter major competitions.

Trying too hard?

For especially talented athletes, fame and fortune follow. Crowds cheer them and newspaper and television reports present them as heroes. However, some athletes, as they struggle to be the best, make mistakes. How serious are these mistakes? Are these athletes still heroes? You decide.

Amazing facts

US golfer Tiger Woods hit his first golf ball when he was only nine months old.

Young children such as these train as gymnasts at sports schools in China. They aim for Olympic gold.

Dimosthenis Tampakos of Greece won a gold medal at the 2004 Olympics.

ATHENS 2004

NS 2004

Jacobellis falls during her Olympic snowboard run and loses gold.

snowboard cross   race involving four or more snowboarders

LINDSEY JACOBELLIS: SNOWBOARDER

At the 2006 Winter Olympics, US athlete Lindsey Jacobellis soared along the twisting snowboard cross trail. She had a 46-metre (50-yard) lead. Victory was hers!

A flashy twist

At the second-to-last jump, in front of the grandstand, she grabbed her snowboard for a flashy mid-air twist . . . and fell. That's when Switzerland's Tanja Frieden sped past to win the gold medal. Jacobellis took silver. She had lost the gold medal for herself and her country.

One snowboarder told reporters that when you have the lead, you add something extra for the crowd – but, he added, "not at the Olympics".

Why did Jacobellis risk gold for a flashy jump? Jacobellis is still a sports star. However, do you think she is a hero?

ZINEDINE ZIDANE: FOOTBALLER

Frenchman Zinedine Zidane (nicknamed Zizou) is one of the greatest athletes in the world. He is a midfielder with a talent for scoring goals.

Captain Zidane

In 2006 Zidane was captain of the French team for the **World Cup**. At age 34, he would retire after this tournament. Zidane led France to the final match against Italy. What an exciting game! France and Italy were tied until Italy finally clinched a narrow victory. However, Zidane was no longer on the pitch. Where was he?

midfielder	player positioned in the middle of the pitch
World Cup	football tournament where the national teams of 32 countries compete to win the World Cup trophy

Zidane (right) scores the first goal of the World Cup final against Italy.

Amazing facts

Zidane became a French hero during the 1998 World Cup, when he led France to a stunning victory over Brazil. He also won the Golden Ball award as the best player of the tournament.

Materazzi falls
down on the field
after being hit
by Zidane.

Zidane's picture was
shown on Paris's Arc de
Triomphe with the words
"Zizou On T'aime." ("We
Love You, Zizou.")

In **extra time**, Italian player Marco Materazzi said something offensive to Zidane. Zidane used his head to knock Materazzi to the ground. Zidane was quickly sent off by the referee.

Placing blame

The next day, the French **sports minister** called Zidane's action "unpardonable". She feared children around the world would copy Zidane.

FIFA, the world football organization, blamed both players. It fined Zidane £3,100 and required him to perform three days of **community service** at a children's hospital. It also fined Materazzi £2,070 and banned him from playing his next two games.

However, Zidane still won the Golden Ball as the tournament's best player. Should he have received the award? What do you think?

community service	work without pay for the benefit of others
extra time	extra period of play to decide the winner of a drawn game
sports minister	government official concerned with sport

Ron Artest: Basketball Player

Ron Artest played basketball for the Indiana Pacers in the United States. When Artest fouled Detroit Piston player Ben Wallace during a game, the two began to fight.

The fight grows

Just as things calmed down, a fan threw a cup of liquid at Artest. Others in the crowd began throwing cups, plastic bottles, and food. Artest charged into the stands and punched a fan. Other Pacers joined the fight and, in all, nine people were treated for minor injuries. Five were taken to hospital.

Amazing facts

Pistons coach Larry Brown said, "It's the ugliest thing I've seen as a coach or player." *People* magazine called the incident "one of the ugliest scenes in NBA history".

| foul | any move or action that is against the rules |

The Pacers' coach and a referee separate Artest (right) and Wallace.

In 2004 Artest played for the Indiana Pacers.

Coaches restrain Artest
after the fight.

Expressing the thoughts of many, the head of the NBA David Stern said, "Players must not enter the stands." The NBA therefore suspended Artest, and he missed 73 games, losing nearly £2.6 million in salary.

Who's to blame?

However, some players understand why Artest did what he did. They say he was protecting himself from fans, who can get out of control.

Should players be judged only by their play on the court, or also by their personal behaviour? Should the fans share the blame for this incident? Did the NBA do the right thing?

Amazing facts

Despite being a superb basketball player, Artest has a history of angry outbursts. In 2002 he threw a 68-kilogram (150-pound) stretching machine. In 2003 he smashed a £51,775 video screen.

Ben Johnson: Olympic Runner

When Canadian athlete Ben Johnson began working with coach Charlie Francis, Francis called him "a skinny, 93-pound runt". Hard work and training turned Johnson into a world-class runner.

Becoming a winner

When he was 19, Johnson competed in the 1984 Olympics. He finished third. Three years later, he set a world record, finishing the 100-metre race in 9.83 seconds. At the 1988 Olympics, Johnson won the gold medal and set another world record.

However, soon after winning the gold, Johnson lost his medal. His world record was also taken away and he was suspended from competition.

Amazing facts

In 1988 the Associated Press, a large news agency, named Johnson the Male Athlete of the Year.

At the 1988 Olympics, Johnson (right) finished first, ahead of US sprinter Carl Lewis.

Police had to guard Johnson on his way back to Canada after the 1988 Olympics.

Why was Johnson punished? Tests showed that he had used **performance-enhancing** drugs. He admitted to taking drugs since the age of 16 because he wanted to be the best. Runner Carl Lewis, who lost the gold medal to Johnson in 1988, believes that Johnson would not have taken drugs without his coach's encouragement.

Drugs and sport

Many athletes have been accused of taking drugs. Some athletes believe that performance-enhancing drugs give them a better chance to win, while others are encouraged by their coaches to take drugs.

How do drugs hurt sport in general? How should cheating athletes be punished?

Amazing facts

At the 2004 Athens Olympics, Asafa Powell of Jamaica ran the 100-metre sprint in 9.77 seconds. This new world record was set without the use of drugs.

performance enhancing something that improves an athlete's natural ability

Jennifer Capriati: Tennis Player

Athlete Jennifer Capriati began playing tennis at the age of three.

Teen wonder

At the age of 13 she signed an **endorsement** deal with a sportswear company worth millions of pounds. She became a professional tennis player. At the age of 16, Capriati was ranked number 7 in the world, and the next year she won Olympic gold.

But then the trouble began. Capriati felt pressured to win.

Amazing facts

Tennis star Serena Williams played her first tournament at age four. By age 10, she had won 46 out of 49 tournaments, and at age 14 she turned **professional**.

endorsement	money made promoting a company's product
professional	in sport, an athlete who plays for money

At the age of 15 Capriati became the youngest semi-finalist ever at Wimbledon, one of the world's major tennis tournaments.

In 1992 Capriati won Olympic gold in Barcelona.

Capriati won the Australian Open in 2001 after her comeback to tennis.

In 1993, at the age of 17, Capriati gave up tennis to finish high school. That December she was charged with shoplifting a cheap ring. At the age of 18 she was arrested for possession of **marijuana**. Friends claimed that Capriati had been using drugs for a year. Two days after her arrest, the former star entered a **drug rehabilitation programme**.

Taking charge

Capriati blamed the pressure of sport. She blamed herself, too, and took a long break from tennis. When she returned, she was stronger and more confident. "I'm in charge now," she said, and in October 2001 she became the number-one ranked female tennis player.

Do you think Capriati is a sports hero? Is her recovery and climb back to the top more heroic than winning gold?

drug rehabilitation programme	**support for people trying to give up drugs**
marijuana	**illegal drug made from the leaves and flowering tops of the hemp plant**

Cathy Rigby: Gymnast

In 1971 US athlete Cathy Rigby won the World Cup championship for gymnastics. The United States had never had a gymnast perform so well, and her win encouraged many other US gymnasts. Rigby won numerous other medals and participated in both the 1968 and 1972 Olympic Games.

Her secret

However, Rigby had a dangerous secret. After her coaches encouraged her to lose weight, Rigby developed **anorexia** and **bulimia**. She felt she had to stay thin in order to win. At the age of 19 Rigby gave up gymnastics, but she continued to battle eating problems for the next 12 years.

Deadly illness

Anorexia can be deadly. US gymnast Christy Henrich died of anorexia in 1994.

Rigby practises her balance beam routine in 1972.

anorexia	eating problem characterized by a failure to eat
bulimia	eating problem characterized by overeating and then purging (vomiting)

In 2005 Rigby played Peter Pan in a show to benefit New York City children.

Rigby became a sports announcer for gymnastics competitions and opened two gymnastics schools of her own. She got married and had two children, but she still suffered from eating problems.

Facing facts

In 1981 Rigby finally faced her disease. She talked to doctors and worked with a counsellor. With hard work and help, she slowly overcame her eating problems.

Is winning more important than everything else? Where should you draw the line? When you look at Rigby today, do you see a heroic survivor?

Good advice

Rigby advises: "Good health is worth a lot more than gold medals. I should have seen my doctor for advice when my coach asked me to lose weight."

YOU DECIDE

Top athletes earn a lot of money. Do athletes deserve the amount of money they make? Why or why not? If not, how much do you think they should make?

What is reasonable?

Top athletes work hard not only on the playing field, but also after the game. They sign autographs, promote products, and participate in charity events. Do you think we expect too much of athletes? Why or why not?

US basketball player Charles Barkley once said, "I don't want to be a **role model**." Should we expect athletes to be good people as well as good athletes? Why or why not?

| role model | person whose behaviour is copied by others |

Golfer Tiger Woods was the world's highest-paid athlete in 2005. He earned £45 million just through sponsorship and **endorsements**.

Glossary

anorexia eating problem characterized by a failure to eat

bulimia eating problem characterized by overeating and then purging (vomiting)

community service work without pay for the benefit of others

drug rehabilitation programme support for people trying to give up drugs

endorsement money made promoting a company's product. Sometimes athletes wear certain clothing because they have an endorsement deal with that clothes company.

extra time extra period of play to decide the winner of a drawn game

foul any move or action that is against the rules

marijuana illegal drug made from the leaves and flowering tops of the hemp plant

midfielder player positioned in the middle of the pitch

performance enhancing something that improves an athlete's natural ability

professional in sport, an athlete who plays for money. Athletes who play for university teams are not considered professional because they are not paid.

role model person whose behaviour is copied by others. Many children see their favourite athlete as a role model.

snowboard cross race involving four or more snowboarders. Snowboard cross became an Olympic sport in 2006.

sports minister government official concerned with sport

World Cup football tournament where the national teams of 32 countries compete to win the World Cup trophy

Want to Know More?

Books

* *The Making of a Champion: A World-Class Gymnast*, Lloyd Readhead (Heinemann Library, 2004)

* *Need to Know: Steroids*, Sean Connoly (Heinemann Library, 2001)

* *On the Edge: Snowboarding*, Chuck Miller (Raintree, 2004)

Websites

* www.fifa.com
  Learn more about football from the world football organization.

* www.iaaf.org
  This site gives up-to-date news about track and field athletics.

* www.itftennis.com
  For the latest information about tennis players and competitions, visit the site of the International Tennis Federation.

If you liked this Atomic book, why don't you try these...?

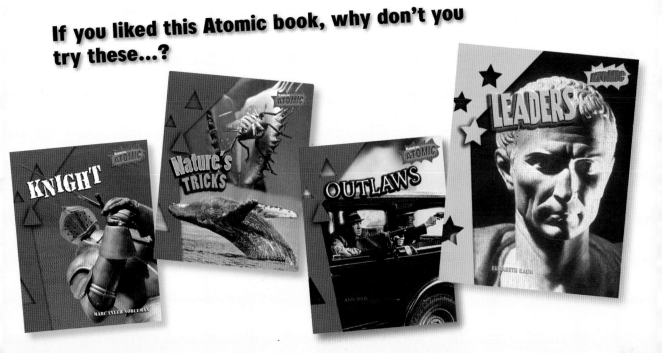

Index

Notes for adults

Use the following questions to guide children towards identifying features of discussion text:

Can you give an example of a statement of the issue on page 4?
Can you find examples of present tense language on page 8?
Can you give examples of different opinions from page 11?
Can you find examples of connectives on page 16?
Can you find an example of summary on page 19?